THE REALITY
OF
MERCY

Kimberly Olson

ISBN 978-1-0980-8519-3 (paperback)
ISBN 978-1-0980-8520-9 (digital)

Christian Faith Publishing, Inc.
832 Park Avenue
Meadville, PA 16335
www.christianfaithpublishing.com

Printed in the United States of America

To my grandchildren, Kane and Eleanor, I thank you for the joy and laughter you have brought to my life. You have given me a better understanding of my purpose. May your eyes always look to the heavens to fill your heart with joy and love. I love you to the moon and back. To my precious husband, I thank you for the encouraging words to move forward and for also having my back, whatever the circumstance.

I have been born again. Born of the spirit, and there is no turning back for me. My past is gone, never to return. My eyes look, and they see the glory that belongs to God. I pray for continued sight as I shed my past and allow the light to become brighter. Today I see an achievable destiny, one of much faith, love, and hope. My God is my destiny. All glory and praise go to him for gifting me with sight. Heavenly Father, thank you for my life, thank you for your patience, thank you for loving me, thank you for sharing your words with such an undeserving sinner, thank you for the mercy you have bestowed upon me. I am humbled to be your child.

Chapter One

High Score

I was abruptly awakened by the sound of a voice. Still a little foggy, I sat up to listen more intently. David was still sleeping, so I knew it was not his voice I had heard. Then I felt that old familiar feeling. The one I get when spending time with God. I was still tired, so I tried ignoring the feeling. It was just too early to get up. I put my head back down on the pillow. What I should have said is "Okay, God, what is the urgency this morning? What is your plan for me today?" My mind started running in overtime. Thoughts were bombarding me from all directions. I knew there was no more sleep for me.

You see, God talks to me. I know for some of you that might be difficult to understand. Believe me, I was one of those unbelievers. For years now I have wondered why God talks to me. Why did he give me the ability to hear him? You will start to understand my pondering as I share a glimpse of my past. It is one I have not shared much because of the ugliness I embraced. So why was I chosen? I am no scholar, I do not have fancy initials behind my name, and I am certainly not a theologian. Yet God has taken me on some wild travels. He once allowed me an out-of-body experience. It was the game changer for me. I still ponder the question of why me. God has all the answers to the questions that perplex me. Little by little, he peals back the answers, but what I have come to realize is I must be prepared to listen. I have this bad habit of being impatient. As a human, I struggle because I always want the answers now. I want my life to make sense. Part of what God has shown me is the answers are in my past. He took me on a journey into that past. He has helped me relive moments of my life. He made it clear they were defining moments. Each moment in time is the moment that has brought me to him. Some were good, many ugly, some uneventful. I had trouble with the rejections and disappointments. I was baffled why I had to go through so many difficult times. God has revealed to me some answers. All my experiences have worked together to give me life. Even though this world is dark, and I lived in the darkness, the light has always been bright. God has helped me out of darkness. I can still see it, but I do not live there.

I am a sinner. If I judged myself as humans tend to do, I would be one of the worst sinners. I did not just come to that conclusion without statistics. I found a formula on how to judge myself. My reference was the Ten Commandments. God gave to us these commandments as a guide for our lives. I decided to award points to each commandment. It is hard for me to share my results, but it will give you insight on how I treated God's authority. You will also see how I concluded that I am one of the worst sinners of all, as seen through the eyes of a human. I used a scale of one to ten to rate myself. Ten being the worst rating one could obtain.

I know God has forgiven me for all my sins regardless of my score. He talks to me; he has restored my soul. It is amazing how he forgives us, yet we have so much trouble forgiving ourselves.

Here is how this is going to work. I will show you the commandment, explain how I treated God's law, and then give you my numerical result. Get prepared; my conclusion is mind-blowing.

Commandment one: Thou shall have no other gods before me

The first forty-five years of my life, I was my own god. In my mind, everything revolved around me. I, I, I, me, me, me. I was self-centered, egotistical, selfish, proud, and my list of words just keeps going. At least you get the idea of my outlook. Those were labels people had given to me. I did not care; labels were just words. They meant nothing to me. I had my own plans, and no one was going to interfere. Looks like a staggering ten points for me. This conclusion came easy. Either God gets the glory, or someone or something else becomes your focus. In my case, I was the god. This is not going to get much prettier. I had my life to live, and that was what I was doing. Living a life for me.

Commandment two: You shall not make for yourself an idol in the form of anything

What does this mean? It means I did not pay attention. I worshipped a lot of images and had many idols. Some of which were money, travel, position, authority (my authority), and of course, fun. I felt any realistic person would want those things. I just wanted them more than most. Those things were my goals, my achievements; they gave me a purpose. For this exam, they also gave me a score of ten.

Commandment three: You shall not misuse the name of the Lord your God

I shudder now just thinking of my stance with this commandment. I am sickened when I think of how I behaved toward God. I never thought about the damage I was doing to myself. More importantly, I never saw the disgrace I placed on our Father's name.

Not much left my lips that did not have a Jesus Christ or God attached. Those names certainly were not spoken in a godly manner. I was out of control, and at the time did not even realize it. I was truly pathetic. There is nothing else to receive but another ten.

Things are not looking too good for me right now. I have a high score, and we just got started.

Commandment four: Remember the Sabbath day, keeping it holy

I worked hard all week. I partied on Saturday night and certainly could not manage to rise early for church on Sunday. The Sabbath was my day to delight in, to do my way. This was the day to enjoy Kim. I was the spotlight of my day. Rack up another ten for me.

Commandment five: Honor your father and mother

As I thought about this one, I felt shameful. I took pride in myself as being a good daughter, but now looking back, was I really? I loved my parents deeply, and I still do. I was heartbroken after my father passed. I am extremely fortunate to still have my mother. At the age of ninety-seven, she is still the kindest person I know.

I still lied to them, I was deceitful, I even took high ground and thought I was superior at times. I told them what I thought in a not-so-pleasant attitude on occasions when I was being reprimanded. What a gem I was. My points are getting out of control, and we are only halfway through. Another ten points for me.

Let us move on. It is not easy looking into your own life. It is much easier to point out someone else's faults and feel good about it. I guess I would get a ten for that also if God were to add another commandment.

Commandment six: Thou shall not murder

I am excited for this one. I can say I never killed anyone. Well, not physically anyway. I thought I was going to earn a one here. God tugged at my heart, opened my eyes, and made me take a bit of time with this one. This is what I saw, and I am sad to admit this. Emotionally, I have destroyed many lives. I took their life without anyone knowing. They continued to be okay on the outside, but I killed them on the inside. How devastating it is to admit to another ten.

Commandment seven: Thou shall not commit adultery

Another commandment I did not live up to. A huge failure for me. Another high score. I am starting to wonder if that was my goal all along. Was I trying to sabotage myself from the beginning?

I started out young, pregnant, immature, yet believed I was wise, ready, and mature. It did not take long before I felt unwise, certainly not ready, and back to being immature. My husband then worked long hours and did not have time for the boys or me. We lived separate lives yet together. Instead of seeking help from wise counsel, I chose my own wisdom. Another bad choice. I had an affair. I had many affairs in my mind, but I finally stepped over the line. I chose myself once again and blamed my husband for what I did. If I could find him today, I would ask for forgiveness. That still does not let me off the hook. I conclude I deserve another ten.

Commandment eight: Thou shalt not steal

The pain just keeps coming. I just could not get it right. This one is simple. Do not mess with something that does not belong to you. Sounds easy. Of course, that is not the road I took. I am not a harden thief, but I am sure stealing is stealing. How many pencils did I take from a classmate? How much money did I take from my parents' drawer so I could buy candy? How about knowing someone else took something and I kept quiet? Probably made me accessory to the fact and guilty. How many times did I take something from work because it was small, and I needed it? I am sure my list is longer, but you get the point. I am guilty. They may seem like small crimes. There is no way around it; the results are the same—stealing. Hate to admit this, but another ten.

Commandment nine: Thou shalt not bear false witness against thy neighbor

There seems to be a common theme here. I am drawn to the number ten. Just keeps popping its ugly head up in my results. Now this commandment I have a story for, but I will just get to the point. I will give you the shortened version: I lied. Cannot get any plainer than that. Oh, look, another ten points for me.

Commandment ten: You shall not covet your neighbor's house. You shall not covet your neighbor's wife, or his manservant or maidservant, his ox or donkey, or anything that belongs to your neighbor

What does it mean to covet? To yearn to possess or have something. Wow. That was me. I wanted what they had. The new car, the new house, the anything I did not have. Even if I had one, I wanted one better than theirs. My life was about big, better, more, and now. Not much of a surprise I get another ten.

Now to the totals. One hundred out of one hundred. It is hard for me to look at that number. It reflects my old life. That number is not me anymore. I thank God for what he has done for me. With him, I am new.

2 Corinthians 5:17. Therefore, if anyone is in Christ, he is a new creation; the old has gone, the new has come!

Looking
in
All
the
Right
Places

What words can I share
With others this day
That will bring them much joy
And help them obey

Our life can be simple
Much love it can bring
The evil must go
Along with its sting

Smiles to our faces
Pureness in our hearts
It is those kinds of changes
That make great starts

We must be our own person
Own up to our faults
It is our God that sees all
He gives to us the results

I love him so dearly
I want that for you too
I pray this day
You make that breakthrough

It is a day you will remember
You will never forget
You will be changed forever
Without any regret

God wants us home
To be by his side
He has given us his word
As a daily guide

Open his word
Feel the difference in you
No more denying
It is God you must pursue

As I lay sleeping in bed that morning, when God abruptly woke me up, I knew he was about to reveal answers to many of my questions. The plan he was sharing was exciting yet terrifying. He let me know there was a purpose for everything in my life. He did not care what my score was. He already knew my score.

God has been merciful to me. I feel unworthy of his mercy. Mercy is something that you do not earn, but you are given even if you do not deserve it. He graciously reminds me I am his child. He loves me. He is everywhere for me. All he wants is my love in return. He wants to hear from me. He wants a relationship with me. He lets me know I can always trust in him.

God has shown me moments of my past. Those moments have helped me put the pieces of my life back together for his glory. They reflect who I was and who I am.

He shares time with me. He places words on my heart. That prompts more questions. What do I do with these words? They come to me as poetry. Do I share them? Are they just for me? Would anyone understand them like I do? Are they just words to occupy my mind for the moment? I cannot answer these questions; only God can. I have tried for some time to ignore the poetry, but with passing days, months, and years, I feel he is insisting today I share them.

Jeremiah 33:3. Call to me and I will answer you and tell you great and unsearchable things you do not know.

Heart
Pieces

I thought I had given
My sins to God
But today I realized
It is just a facade

It is time to ask God
To search my heart
Unlock the compartments
So I can depart

Depart from a past
That anchors me down
I feel so often
I just might drown

The facts of my life
Sure, are not pretty
I need to move on
I must stop all the pity

The truth is important
The facts are the facts
I must humble myself
To make an impact

Prayer must become
My pillar for life
It will help you and me
To love without strife

The battles are many
My prayers must ring out
I cannot delay
I must stay devout

I give God my sin
I will not take it back
I must be a warrior
I will make a comeback

My family is in trouble
I hear their laughter
My prayers must continue
In hopes of giving
them a thereafter

Free in Love

This is where
My story begins
Jesus Christ died
For my sins

He went to heaven
To watch over me
He gave me the ability
To be free

It took me a while
To know what that means
But now I know
It has become a routine

I look outside
My four small walls
And see if anyone
Has taken a fall

It does not take long
To see the broken
I am humbled to be
One of God's spokesmen

The cross is a symbol
Of God's love for them
It gives me a chance
To become their friend

It is a gesture of love
To help them feel
Their life is more
Than just an ordeal

God places us
On his path
Here we will work
On his behalf

The Gospel
Is my job to share
So no one will ever
Have to be in despair

I love my God
He brings me peace
Now I pray for you
To find his relief

He
Exists

My eyes are focused
They see the holy one
They know his glory
They see what he has done

My life depends on the focus
I must look straight ahead
It is my lifeline
My spirit will never be dead

Each night darkness enters
But my eyes are on the light
There is nothing I cannot do
If I keep him in my sight

He cleanses my heart
Of all I have done wrong
He leaves me full of joy
He makes me so strong

My faith is in him
For I know he exists
Some say he does not
But I must insist

I have lost my loved ones
Their backs are to me
I cannot change my focus
For Jesus set me free

He loves me more than ever
He listens to my heart
My life keeps getting better
He gave to me a new start

Jesus is my Savior
He saved me from this world
He can save you also
You just say the word

Lay your old self down
Give Him what is due
Never look back
Your life will now be new

My poems reflect life. Many share the journey of a lost sinner. Some of a sinner being found. God revealed to me that there are many others, just like my old self, that need to be found. They are living out my old life. I was one of the fortunate ones who were able to escape the bondage that Satan had placed on me. You may feel your score is too high to be forgiven, but I am proof that theory holds no water. It is time to flee from your past, take up the cross, and follow our Savior Jesus Christ.

Luke 9:23. Then he said to them all: "Whoever wants to be my disciple must deny themselves and take up their cross daily and follow me."

Die
to
Self

I love my Jesus
But what does that mean?
How do I show it?
Is my life just routine?

Have I died to self?
Has my new self come to life?
Am I living in two worlds?
Still living a daily fight

This world is dark and ugly
It wants to keep me here
But my Jesus gives me hope
He makes it truly clear

No longer am I in darkness
Jesus lives in my heart
I get to see his daily light
Darkness must depart

His light is within me
It comes with commands
It's the study of his word
That we need to understand

Many words are in his book
I must read them every day
They nourish and strengthen
They teach me how to pray

Once you accept him
Your heart will be his
A heaviness is lifted
It is just who he is

Close your eyes to darkness
Ask Jesus into your life
He will lead you gently
He will reopen your eyes

I pray for you
To do what's right
You will never regret it
Jesus will give you new life

Daily Struggles

Today's a new day
I must get on track
My eyes must be open
To avoid an attack

God needs me to listen
Slow down a bit
It is him I must follow
To him I must submit

I humble myself
I stop my frustration
Focus on God
Hear his explanation

I know my God
He has a plan for me
But the devil keeps attacking
God, please make him flee

He is a constant annoyance
He tries to make me stray
God, do not allow that
He must go away

My God knows my needs
I cannot survive without him
I must stay humble
Pray away the sin

My heart is clear now
My mind is free
It is God up in heaven
That has done that for me

Out of Control

My faith grows stronger
I want to be used
To lift the souls
Of those that are bruised

So many lives
Are out of control
They follow this world
Right into a sinkhole

Satan is evil
He lurks in the corner
He insists he is from here
But he is a foreigner

He offers his way
Of dishonesty and greed
So many get on board
And off they speed

The longer they are with him
The blacker their life gets
They spin and they spin
But have no regrets

It is my job to share with them
That my Jesus lives
They must know his way
It is life he gives

Our time here is short
We must get it right
Come out of the dark
Step quickly into the light

God will provide
All that you need
It is a wonderful thing
It is his promise he
has guaranteed

Loyalty

I cannot let them fool me
My guard must be up
My position of loyalty
I cannot give up

God is my master
The one I obey
My heart cannot be tempted
I do not want to stray

I wrap my heart
With God's word
My faith will be strong
Whatever is heard

They cannot hurt me now
I am protected by him
I must keep his light on
I will not let it go dim

I pray for peace
To come this day
So all will experience it
Without any dismay

I place my children
In God's hands
He will help them to handle
All his plans

I must not think
I know better
I give him control
So we can work together

I was given a choice that morning. I could do as God was asking, or just ignore him. I could continue my sleep and miss out on my next adventure with him, or I could rise to his call. As you can see, I chose my God. I got up, forgot about the sleep I wanted, headed straight to my prayer room. I removed all my own thoughts. I turned my mind over to him. I gave him the control.

Some of the memories we shared stung, some made me laugh, some painful, and some brought much love to my heart. I pray my life will help lead you to a closer relationship with Christ. Many of my own questions have been answered. I can see how each moment of my life led me to him. I am now usable. I have become his hands and feet. Do not get me wrong, I still fail. The difference now is I repent. My heart hurts when I fail. God shows his mercy, and he picks me up. I dust myself off, get back on the narrow path, and pick up my cross daily.

Matthew 7:13. "Enter through the narrow gate. For wide is the gate and broad is the road that leads to destruction, and many enter through it."

Cry Out for Mercy

The Lord will rescue me
I must cry out
He is waiting to hear my voice
That is what it's all about

I feel so helpless
I feel so weary
This world I live in
Is extremely eerie

I took the wrong road
The path was wide
It is easy to get lost
So many places to hide

I lived in the dark
There was no light
I stumbled and fell
Most every night

I hid my shame
I lied to myself
I have no one to blame
Except oneself

God's path is narrow
I need to focus on him
He is my light in the darkness
With him I will win

What Is Wealth

How simple my life is
One of little wealth
But one of great value
One of much health

I choose to stand
With God's only Son
There is nothing with him
I cannot get done

He stands with me
All day and night
He helps me to navigate
His path with his light

I have swayed from his path
Caused myself much pain
He waits in the shadows
For me to refrain

If a battle goes on
Within my mind
He is there to help me
He wants to keep me aligned

I am humbled to know
He loves me so
It is a love that I will keep
I will never outgrow

I close my eyes
I wait for the feeling
His arms hold me tight
I can feel his healing

I thank God above
For sending his Son
It is a day that brought life
I certainly have won

Release the Burden

Today I sit
I wonder why
I fight against
My God so high

He comes to help me
Throughout the day
He just wants to guide me
Send me on my way

I pray for wisdom
I must be a better person
I must stop hurting myself
With excess burden

I read his word
I take it in
There's not much I want
Except not to sin

It's easy to accomplish
I need to get it done
I must focus on my God
I must focus on his Son

My days will be bright
Full of light
He will fill my soul
With so much delight

I love my time
When I am alone with God
He helps me conquer sin
I beat all the bad odds

God's patient and loving
He is kind as can be
He is given me everything
Now I will succeed

My Bond

I wonder what God
Has in store for me
I must build my relationship
I have a need to see

Relationships are not easy
They require much care
I must give it my all
I must be fair

I must never see myself
Coming in first
If that is what I see
I certainly will be cursed

My bond must be deep
I must carry much trust
My heart must be filled
With love not lust

The love and the trust
Are built upon faith
It makes my days
Feel so safe

God wants to hear from me
Every day
It is easy to do
I must bow down and pray

His visits give to me
A chance to do better
He helps me to pour out
His love in a letter

He places his thought
On my mind to share
I know one day
It will help someone prepare

The one true God
Is the love of my life
He is here for us
He gives his advice

Take that first leap of faith
Build a bond with him
His arms will bring peace
It will be difficult to sin

This is the relationship
You must build together
It is one that will last
Into the forever

I have made God number one in my life. Of course, that was not always the case with me. I know now with him by my side, no one can bring me down. My sight has changed as the years have gone by. My focus is on him alone. I see beauty that has been disguised by Satan, I see ways to help instead of judging, I see children blossoming before my eyes instead of hindering me. I feel alive, and I want to move forward instead of standing still. My relationship with God belongs to me. I will not let anyone take it from me. They cannot diminish it. I take ownership of it.

It takes work, hard work, to keep a relationship alive. It is not a one-sided job. The definition of a relationship is "the way in which two or more concepts, objects, or people are connected, or the state of being connected."

People have said to me they are not religious. I say great! I'm not talking about religion; I'm talking about a relationship. If you are new to this concept or still sitting on the fence about Jesus, I pray you will continue with an open mind. Somewhere in these pages, God has a message for you. Please look, take your time, and do not hurry yourself. I promise you will not be disappointed. If I try to hurry my life, do not take my time with God, I become lost. I found that to be true one early fall morning.

Deuteronomy 31:6. Be strong and courageous. Do not be afraid or terrified because of them, for the Lord your God goes with you; he will never leave you nor forsake you.

The Ride

Keys in my hand
Purse on my shoulder
I wondered what was missing
It was my beholder

Thought I was ready
To get on my way
But without him beside me
I was about to stray

A sense of heaviness
Weighed on my heart
As I got in the car
Ready to depart

I looked at the seat
Next to me
I realized it was empty
Then I heard his plea

He asked me to bring him
Whatever the cost
So I would never feel
That I was lost

A tear hit my lap
My head now bowed
The silence was deafening
Yet so very loud

I hurried my life
This morning for what
I did it my way
And took a shortcut

God wants our attention
All through the day
He sends us messages
Along the way

I know he is with you
He has touched you too
You must open your heart
To know his cue

He loves you, my family
It is the best feeling ever
Let him offer you a ride
Into the forever

I was so disappointed in myself that morning as I set out to leave. I was in a hurry and decided my prayer time would come later. I gave God the back seat to me.

I am better than that, yet I allowed this world to suck me in. It's not an easy life God hands to you once you accept Christ. He never promised us a life full of bliss and roses. He has made it clear we will be in battle for our salvation. Satan will rise his nasty head into your business every occasion he can muster.

That morning as I sat in my car, I realized I had left Christ home. My world consisted of me. I never left that day. I went back inside after a long sobbing session. I brought my Jesus with me, and we talked until I had it right. At least for that day, I was where I needed to be. Remember, daily we must pick up the cross. Each morning is another choice. Some days I stumble. My falling has become less as the years go by, but I am not perfect. The word "perfect," it was made for my Jesus. Nothing is perfect except for him. I find my peace in that. I find peace in the fact that my Father in heaven loves me and I him. He is my helper, my strength. He saves me from myself and this world.

1 John 4:7–8. Dear Friends, let us love one another, for love comes from God. Everyone who loves has been born of God. Whoever does not love does not know God, because God is love.

God's Face

I hear a knock
I let him in
He looks around
He sees I have sinned

He places me gently
Before his face
He waits for me
To plead my case

The words I use
Are just an excuse
I must hear myself speak
And stop the abuse

My relationship with God
Is important to me
I must look in his eyes
Understand his decree

His words are so simple
They carry eternal life
They are given to me
For such a small price

Love his Son
Live by his word
It is a simple command
And one that I have heard

I ask for forgiveness
Tell him I love him so
I have managed to skirt
Another death blow

The Joy of the Spirit

God never promised me
A life full of bliss
He did promise me
A way to exist

It is the love of his Son
That will carry me through
On those days that are hard
When I feel blue

His Son came to save me
As well as you too
We must stand with our faith
To him we must be consistently true

It is my job to pass
God's word along
Some want to hear it
Some think I am wrong

It is not about what they think
It is about the spirit within
When the spirit is lit
You will no longer want to sin

I am sorry if you disagree
No pain have I caused
The love of the Lord lives in me
He I must applaud

Time Spent Wisely

As I pray to my God
Distractions abound
Evil tries to win me
I hold my own ground

My voice starts to rise
My God brings me peace
There is nothing evil can do
To make me cease

I smile to myself
Knowing evil cannot win
He digs in deep
Yet I refuse to sin

When I speak to my God
He protects my soul
There is no penetrating me
My God has control

It is a peaceful place
In the presence of God
Some find it challenging
Some find it odd

For me, his grace
Comes during prayer
I rejoice in this time
That we get to share

I pray for you
Give God some time
He will grant you grace
He will do away with your crime

My Master

Sin is not my master
The love for Jesus controls me
Jesus opened many doors
He has set my spirit free

I see a sliver of darkness
It tries to embrace my mind
What a mistake darkness makes
The light cannot be outshined

Darkness is only a memory
It is about my past
The light gave me new life
I have been recast

The best part of me is light
The light and I are one
I get to feel the warmth inside
My Jesus and I have won

Sometimes we sit in silence
I get to enjoy his peace
I love those special moments
I pray they never cease

Jesus died to save me
He took my sins that day
His life lives within me now
My master I obey

Precious Jesus, my life is yours
Do as you see fit
Use me for your purpose
I will never ever quit

Notes of Color

Many notes are on my wall
They are messages for you
I pray you get to read them
Help me make it through

I know it is not about me
It is about what I must do
My direction gets messed up
I must turn to see your view

My focus has been foggy
My eyes have been blurred
I cannot see beyond myself
I listen for your word

I sit in silence
I cry your name out loud
My heart seems so hardened
How did I get so proud?

Why don't I understand
What you have for me
I feel I do not fit anywhere
Only you have the key

Today more notes
I placed them on my wall
It is my cry for help
Father, do you hear my call?

I need you more than ever
Do you still want me?
Fix my broken pieces
Once again, I want to see

I know you are the answer
My face is on the ground
I plead my case to you
I pray I am found

Chapter Two

The Gentle Touch

I think it is important to understand how I got to this point in my life. It is an accumulation of minutes, hours, days, and years. It was how I thought or the lack of thinking that has gotten me here. I never realized that God touched me and stood beside me daily. That was the lie this world wanted me to believe. Satan was doing his job well. He kept me in the dark so I would not notice who was with me. He is weak and sneaky, but he could not keep me down.

Once my eyes were opened, I found direction, focus, and a love that compares to nothing earthly. My God has never left me. He was with me even when I chose not to give him the glory.

How do you know when you are touched? It is a feeling. A spiritual inner feeling. One that there is no other explanation for. God took me on this journey into my past for a purpose. He opened my eyes. He pulled many memories from files I had closed or had not thought of for a long time. Now with my eyes open, I know God saved me. He brought peace and comfort to a sinner. I thank God for the awareness of my past. I thank him for holding my hand as I looked back on my past. Thank you, God, for showing me the light.

This is my first memory of being touched by God:

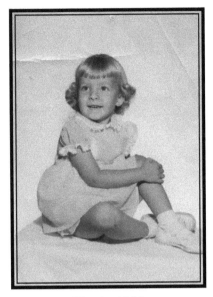

Kim in 1958

It was September 1958, a couple of days before my fifth birthday. I was quite excited that morning. It was my first day of kindergarten. I remember so many things about that day. The sun was shining. There was a warm breeze. My mom drove me to school.

She and I had visited my classroom the week before, so I had no fear. I knew my teacher. I knew how to navigate the halls. I even knew where I was sitting in the classroom.

There was only one problem that morning—my mom was running late. She dropped me off in front of the school. She gave me the biggest smile, told me to enjoy my day. She said she was looking forward to hearing about it later that evening. She trusted me to go to my class. I did exactly that.

It did feel strange once I walked in. The halls were empty, I heard nothing. I was determined to be brave, so I continued to my room. I was surprised when I entered to find no one there. I sat down thinking that at any moment, my teacher would arrive. A lot of time went by. I pulled my rug out and lay down. That's when I fell apart.

I was scared. The room was dark, and I had no idea how to turn the lights on. I started to get chilled even though it was warm outside. The floodgates opened. I sobbed and cried out for help. Within a few minutes, I felt someone touch my hair. They caressed it. The warmth came back to my body. I stopped crying out. It was a crazy experience because no one was there, but I felt someone.

Shortly after that, a woman entered the room. Her face showed surprise to see me. I, on the other hand, was excited to see her. She was the office lady. She brought me back to her room. She called my mom to come get me. You see, I arrived a week early. I guess mom was a little confused about the start date. Mom came and picked me up. I explained what happened in that classroom, but she said the feeling was my imagination playing tricks on me. I believed that for decades.

It may seem to you that I imagined the feeling also. I would have agreed with you in my younger years, but now I know Jesus. I know what he can do. I see what he does today.

I can recall so many times being touched and yet no one was there. The truth is someone was and is there. It is our Savior. He has always been with me. I did not allow my senses to dive deep enough to understand the feeling. Remember, I was my own god. Things just happened without a reason in my old life.

Just like the office woman. She never knew she was sent to save me. I do remember her telling my mom she was on her way out, leaving for the day. She said she got this feeling to check on the classroom I was in. Coincidence? I believe that is a made-up word. Everything has a purpose and a reason. God spoke to her without her even being aware. I think one day, God will share that memory with her and reward her for being faithful.

Satan thought he was going to score a win for his team. He thought he could play with my mind. Only God knows what would have happened if I was not found by that sweet lady. My God took charge and put Satan in his place.

Psalm 32:8. I will instruct you and teach you in the way you should go; I will counsel you and watch over you.

Are
You
Lost

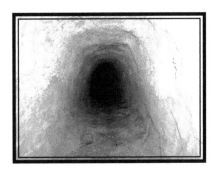

When the flesh rises up
Darkness prevails
God's not around
We have lost his trail

Our minds become weary
Our hearts become cold
We are not who we should be
We become uncontrolled

I watch as this world
Goes down that path
I pray for my family
They never see God's wrath

So many believe
There is no God
Oh, how their thoughts
Are so flawed

Our God watches over us
He sees it all
His heart must break
As he sees us fall

Christians wake up
Pass the Gospel along
Do not give up
We must stay strong

There is one way out
To have faith in our Lord
You must strive for the faith
Continue to move forward

Our days are numbered
They will come to an end
Help those in need
To become God's friend

Focus Change

God came beside me
On this very day
To change my focus
He wants me to be okay

He knows my pain
He feels it too
Between you and me
He is the one to get me through

My focus must change
Satan cannot win
He dealt me a card
Hoping I would sin

Words spoken in anger
Will not set things right
I must do like my Jesus
I must show his light

I talked to my Father
I took his advice
I changed my focus
I do not want to pay a price

He calms my emotions
His love sets me free
I am back on track
For his life is the key

Other Days

God is my everything
He has made me new
He loves me dearly
He keeps me from being blue

He sits with me every day
He listens to my words
Some days I get to hear him
I love when that occurs

I retreat to "our" special room
Where it is just him and me
We spend hours together
It is there I get set free

I bottle so much up inside
I truly do not know why
I try to live in the past
It is there I want to die

My past is so tainted
I hate the things I have done
The only way to rid my past
Is faith in my God's Son

I sit quietly
In hopes I will hear
What he has to say to me
Because He is my cure

I could not live another day
If it was just me alone
Evil would have his way
All I could do is groan

I will live other days
My days will never cease
Each day will get brighter
For my God brings me peace

By the Grace of God

I struggled with my prayers
Looking for words to say
I have been given many blessings
What is wrong with me today?

God knew what was happening
He lifted me from the depths
He has given to me nature
So I can reflect

The rain was gently falling
The birds sang their song
Then out of nowhere
Sprang an animal that
did not belong

He tiptoed across the lawn
He gazed upon my face
His eyes did not leave me
My heart felt warm with grace

It sounds a little crazy
But with God in the mix
All things are possible
The fox was my fix

He made sure I was watching
The reason was unclear
I reached for my camera
In a blink he disappeared

I knew at that moment
God needed my focus
He sent me a message
So I would take notice

I let go of my troubles
My prayers began to flow
God always amazes me
He continues to help me grow

Little Pack

Who am I?
Do I really matter?
Am I only taking up space?
My heart feels it will shatter

I move about freely
But am I really free?
I carry so much baggage
Filled with heavy debris

I try to give it away
But I keep taking it back
The weight is killing me
I feel I'm under attack

I see so many in my boat
Our boat is weighed down
The waterline keeps rising
I feel we will surely drown

I throw my bags off the boat
They float across the surface
I watch them and wonder
Did they ever have a purpose?

My heart beats fast
I am scared to see them go
That baggage is who I am
How can I continue to grow?

I heard a voice
It was directed to me
Keep facing forward
You will be set free

I still struggle daily
Sometimes I want to turn back
But my baggage is gone
God has given me a
different pack

My pack is the Bible
I open it to see
My life can still be a struggle
But with him I know I am free

Life's Increase

My heart is overflowing
God has done this for me
His power is magnificent
It has set my body free

I never expected a
change of heart
That is what makes it so special
He swoops in at any time
It is never accidental

I give thanks to Him
For loving this sinner
He has given me life
I am a winner

My eyes must stay alert
I must look to the light
It brings me much focus
I know I will be alright

Closing my eyes brings darkness
I lived there for so long
I am thankful for my Jesus
For undoing all my wrong

I see what is happening
Many choose the dark
The world is imploding
The devil has made his mark

I no longer am afraid
The light has brought me peace
I sit in total contentment
Knowing my life will
only increase

I thank God for giving me the opportunity to look back into my past. That first day of kindergarten could have had a negative effect on me. Instead, it is my first true memory of being touched and watched over by our God. He provided comfort, peace, and someone to lend a hand to a lost child.

I do not recommend looking into your past too often, unless God has something to share about that past. He gave me a glimpse of himself right there in that dark, cool classroom. I was blessed without even recognizing it at the time or for many years after. All glory and honor go to God.

Psalm 96:2–3. Sing to the Lord, praise his name; proclaim his salvation day after day. Declare his glory among the nations, his marvelous deeds among all peoples.

Moving On

My Heavenly Father
Come close to me
My story is one
That might help others in need

With darkness gone
It leaves me with light
My soul is free
Now I love what is right

I feared myself
I was the "I am"
My hole was deep
I was living a scam

The pain I caused
Hurt others and me
Shattered my soul
The soul I need

The pieces were many
I could not see
How to put them together
In any degree

I had no connection
My eyes could not see
The only thing I truly needed
Certainly was not me

I was granted grace
And by grace alone
My pieces came together
Because of your throne

My back is now turned
I will not live in my past
My face faces forward
This is how one will last

My heart is now open
My ears can hear
I listen intently
For your words that are dear

I love the warmth
You send my way
It humbles me so
Every day

My soul is free
I think of thee
I love you, dear Father
I no longer want to flee

I fear no death
For I am alive
Your Son came to save me
I will now survive

How good it feels
To see the light
I thank you, my Father
For giving me new sight

Lessons

I must not dwell on time
I realize it is short
My time is speeding by
I ask God for his support

Today I pray
My sins go away
God to humble me
As I go about my day

God's spirit lives deep
He is in my soul
He has given to me
All the control

I have the instructions
In a book of much age
It is of no good
If I do not engage

I turn to the Word
Written so long ago
God's Word has not changed
I want you to know

The lessons of life
Are there in his Word
We must read it out loud
So it can be heard

My Day

One day, sweet God
I pray we meet
I will fall
Before your feet

My heart will love
I will feel no pain
For you are the true God
I will always remain

My heart will fill with joy
I will be with you
Oh, what a day
When it finally comes true

I dream of a home
In the heavenly skies
You on your throne
I do not die

Cannot wait to get there
Please understand
I am grateful to thee
For all you have planned

Your patience, your mercy
The help I received
Have led me to you
I will always believe

You are my Savior
My home far away
Soon will come my time
With you I will spend my day

Chapter Three

A Loner

As a child, I was a loner. Not that I chose that for myself, but it was my reality. We lived on a farm in the country. Our neighbors were few and far between. I learned to rely on me.

I was part of a family of seven. I was the youngest child, with seven years between my next sibling and myself. My four siblings were close in age. That left me on my own most of the time. I had to improvise. I went looking for friends. What I found was the comfort of a furry four-legged friend. Her name was Queeny. She was a beautiful German shepherd farm dog. She loved me as much as I loved her. We explored the fields together every day. We would sit by the train track and just wait to wave to the engineer and the brakeman. They became my friends. They always shared a wave and a small toot. I certainly loved the sound of the ten-o'clock train coming. I believe Queeny did too. She always barked, and her tail would wag. It was the highlight of our day.

When we were not in the fields or waiting for the train, we would spend time in her house. We both fit simply fine. It was there that she would listen so intently to my every word. She would cuddle close to me when I was sad and crying. She was gentle. She would kiss my tears away. She was my best friend.

Queeny and I were inseparable. I remember the summer between my second and third grade. It was a hot one. This one night, I could hardly sleep. As the early morning hour came around, things cooled off a little, and I fell back to sleep. I slept much later than normal. It was my job to feed Queeny. I overslept, and I knew she must be hungry. Quickly, I got her food ready. I was sure she would be at the back door waiting, but to my surprise, she was not there. I thought maybe she slept in too because of the heat. She was not in her house. I called her, but no sign of her anywhere. I looked in our special places. I went to the tracks, down the hill to the old water pump, and checked out the old boxcar on the back of our property. No Queeny. Panic rose in me. I just started running and yelling her name.

My dad stopped me. He told me not to worry. He said dogs like to go visit other dogs, and he was sure she would be back soon. I took up camp on the front lawn. From there, I could see quite a distance in three directions. Occasionally, I would call out. If she was lost, she could hear me and follow my voice back home.

The next day, I retraced my steps from the day before. My days were spent looking, calling, and crying. I refused to stop looking. On day four, my hope started to dwindle; my heart was heavy. How could this be. I was alone again. I sat crying, begging for her to appear. Then through wet tears, I saw something in the distance. There was something strange slumbering down our gravel road. I knew it was her. She was looking for me. Where had she been? What happened to her?

She had gotten her head stuck in a bucket. Apparently, she was lapping up the last few drops of milk at the bottom. She spent four days wandering the countryside with that bucket on her head. I ran down the gravel road calling her name. She knew she was found. I knew my friend had returned.

As a small child, God provided me with a best friend. He gave to me someone that brought comfort and love. Again, this is not coincidence. It is real. We have a God that knows just what we need and when we need it. God provides. Our understanding of provisions or how we might want to be provided for may not be the same, but he will provide what you need.

Philippians 4:19. And my God will meet all your needs according to his glorious riches in Christ Jesus.

Precious Friends

My best friends are furry
Some big, some small
They love me for me
Is what I recall

I remember a doghouse
Big and white
It is where Queeny seemed
To make everything right

She listened for hours
Sat by my side
I enjoyed her company
With her I would confide

Many days were lonely
I needed to cry
She brought me a smile
She stopped the sigh

My heart deeply missed her
When she went home
But she is in a great place
She will never be alone

Many a friend
I have had since then
But none like my Queeny
That helped me mend

Today the "girls"
Light up my day

I certainly would miss them
If they went away

They cuddle so close
Both day and night
They listen to me
With much delight

God's opened my mind
To reminisce of this gift
He opened my heart
To give me a lift

I felt kind of sad
Early today
But God and my girls
Have sent the sadness away

They have given me a smile
My heart feels warm
God certainly sent them
So I can beat the storm

They are different than me
They walk on four feet
But the pleasure they bring
Is oh so sweet

I thank God
For giving me these friends
Because their love
Goes on and never ends.

Don't Worry About Me

I rise to the sunshine
My heart feels the joy
It is going to be a great day
One evil cannot destroy

My focus is up
My eyes to the sky
They look for my Jesus
From him I receive my supply

What a glorious day
What a blessed beginning
I rise to no worry
Team Jesus is winning

My spirit is in a twitter
Singing praises to the Lord
My heart is content
It has been restored

I give thanks to my God
For showing me his way
His light lives within me
He is here to stay

I pray for you this day
Salvation you do achieve
It is quite simple for you
You simply need to believe

Become part of one body
We work well together
Any obstacle in the way
We can all weather

Jesus will lead you
To eternity beyond
Your job today
Is to please respond.

Chapter Four

The Beginning of a Hardened Heart

My school days have proven to hold many defining moments. My first day of kindergarten was the first godly embrace I remember. A good memory. The next defining moment God showed me was a trip back to fourth grade. That year caused many tears, embarrassment, and humiliation. It was also the beginning of a hardened heart. I formed a barrier around my heart. I learned from my teacher to rely on me. She taught me to trust no one. Especially not her. At nine years old, I learned many worldly tips. None of them to my advantage. Over the years, I blamed that teacher for my untrusting behavior. I learned to keep everyone at a distance and trusted only myself. It was quite a turning point for me. I became an adult in a child's body.

What I know now is I had never been introduced to Jesus. I thought that this world was about me and them. I had a survival instinct that led me down many rocky roads. The further I followed on that path, the darker it became. I was always looking for something but never sure what it was. My heart seemed to have a hole in it even though I had built this impenetrable shield. I was always looking, finding, but never satisfied. I had a need for more, but I never knew what the more was.

My teacher that year is what we would call a bully. Even though I had never had her as a teacher yet, I had many encounters with her.

None of which were positive. I was dreading the summer ending. I knew this year was going to bring trouble. I had not even stepped foot into my class, and I knew my life was about to change.

Every year, we would come back after summer break and share our summer experiences with our classmates. Mine was always the same. Queeny and I exploring our world. Seems my classmates got tired of hearing about my precious friend. They spoke about their vacations, their long visits with family, and the shopping spree for new school clothes. We had no extra money for things like that. I hated being poor.

I had decided to make this year better. I was going to tell one of the best lies ever. I made up a story about an elaborate trip I had taken with my grandmother. It was supposed to make me feel good. Instead, it brought me the most humiliation I could imagine.

My teacher knew my family and our circumstances. She knew I was lying to my classmates.

She called me to the front of the class. She turned to me with a smirky smile and said, "Okay, tell everyone about your trip and show them pictures if you have some." She knew there was no trip, no pictures, but still she continued asking questions. I had no answers for them. I did not research my lie. I felt my face turn red, tears were whelming in my eyes, and she began to laugh. She said, "You can now take your seat, you little liar." She added, "Just remember you will never have any friends because of who you are."

That was the blow that left a scar for some thirty-six years. I reflected on those words continually. I believed them and was about to prove her right.

I was not the only lost soul that year. I remember a boy, William Reinbold, who seemed to be more withdrawn than me. No one would talk to him, let alone play with him.

Recess time was always brutal for him. No one wanted him on their team. I remember vividly the day my name got pulled out of a hat to be a captain. I got to choose my team. I knew exactly what I was going to do. My first choice was William. This poor boy was always chosen last. When I called his name, he did not move. He was kicking at the dirt on home base. He assumed he was going to be last, so he never paid attention. I called his name a second time. Now the look on his face was priceless. He ran over, gave me a high five, and was ready to play. He was so excited; we were not prepared for what was about to happen. I chose my second player, and they refused to join us. My teacher agreed they did not have to be on our team. Not one other child would play on our team. They called him names. They told him he should go home. What happened next was the battle of all battles. He began to cry. I think that gave him more power. Both arms were swinging like crazy. Anyone in his way took some hard blows. It was chaos.

Just think if my teacher would have done the right thing. That day would have ended so differently. Instead, another blow to an already-defeated little boy.

I retreated into myself deeper after that day. William and I never spoke about what happened. We never spoke about anything. Our eyes would meet most every day, and we would have some intense conversations with sight alone. I wanted to help him, but I just did not know how to do that. I had so many of my own troubles. Remember I was only nine.

That year has played a major role in my life. I allowed one person, my teacher, to change me. I gave her words power over the direction I took. I believed her and continued to be friendless.

As my school years continued, I became stronger. That was my perception at the time. I stood on my own set of principles. They seemed to work for me. I did follow rules. They were my rules. Rule one: No one was going to rule me. Rule two: Always refer to rule one. What more did I need? I was in control of my destiny.

My attitude took me into some painful places. I continued down that path for many years. I put the blame on my teacher. I let her control my destiny. I believed her words. I gave her my control. It took me four decades to regain what I had given to her. I kicked relationships to the curb. I never took time for them. I lived inside myself. Yes, I functioned on the outside, I became strong, I lead, I forged ahead, but with no goal and no friend. What did I really have? That is a question God has answered for me. Today I am free of the excess baggage. For our God is merciful.

Today is the day for you to release your baggage. God is waiting to hear from you.

I pray for my enemies. My teacher was one of the unsuspecting enemies in my life. I pray she was able to repent and find her peace in our Savior Jesus Christ.

As for William, he never did find a friend. It is my understanding that he has not found our Savior either. He racked up a long history of violent crimes against women. According to an officer of the Illinois State Police, he said I was fortunate to be one of William's few surviving victims. I assume he grabbed me that warm summer day to do harm to me, but for a moment we shared what I hope is to be our last intense look into each other's eyes. I think, at that moment, he remembered the kindness I had shown him as a child and the exchange of conversation we shared with our eyes. He allowed me to run, even though he could have finished the job he came to do. You see he is a serial killer. He now resides in an Illinois penitentiary for the crime of murder. I sometimes wonder if I would have befriended him, would so many lives have been changed?

There is a lesson to be learned. Please do not ever turn your back on the lonely, the hurting, and the unloved. You just might be who God had sent to save them.

1 Peter 3:9. Do not repay evil with evil or insult with insult. On the contrary, repay evil with blessing, because to this you were called so that you may inherit a blessing.

Haters

I shudder and shake
Deep from within
That the world we live in
Is so full of sin

Our values we seem
To have kicked to the curb
It is all about us
And being superb

I watched in the background
As laughter erupted
As the horrid remarks
Were so corruptive

Someone they knew
Nothing of at all
Became the victim
And took the fall

I wonder how brave
They will be
When time comes for them
To look at thee

A simple command
Like love thy neighbor
Has gone by the wayside
We have become such haters.

A Different Plan

Do you have a Savior?
Do you spend your days with him?
Has darkness overtaken your mind?
Do you follow his every whim?

I was terrified every day
I was living in the dark
Dark shadows hung over me
It seemed I had been marked

There was a different plan for me
But I had to see the light
I made a choice and turned from dark
I wanted my life to be right

God's Word is where I need to be
It fills my heart and soul
It is there I find my wisdom
My Jesus is the goal

I pray for family and my friends
And those I do not know
I pray they look for the light
I pray their response is not slow

Deafness Within

I cannot hear you
I feel lost and scared
My heart's gone astray
It needs to be repaired

I am always searching
For what I do not know
I wish I could hear you
I need your help to grow

I want to be helped
Yet I sit in doubt
My heart is so lacking
It is you I am without

I have many questions
The answers I lack
My heart's not working
I am on the wrong track

I want to be found
At least I think I do
There is only one way
It is you I must pursue

Your words are not hidden
They are in plain sight
I must encourage my heart
To get it right.

Fallen Truth

Where oh where
Has God's truth gone?
He made it so plain
So we would stand strong

It comes in a simple
Form to read
But many people
They prefer to lead

He has given us free will
To do as we please
We need to remember
He can always foresee

We struggle with trials
We brought on ourselves
The blame comes so easy
But the truth overwhelms

Our fingers they point
In most every direction
Except pointing up
For the perfect correction

We have taken the truth
We boiled it down
We have stripped our God
Of even his crown

Life can be simple
If we live by his truth
Battles would be gone
Life would not be aloof

Seems so strange
We destroy what is true
Just so we can
Have no clue

Our Lord, he is coming
What a fuss there will be
Judgment and righteousness
Will be handed to you and to me

The truth will stand tall
For all to see
It will be quite scary
For those that disagree

Many have lived their lives
By lies alone
Now they will find
They will not be taken home

Chapter Five

The Seed

Life has thrown me many curveballs. Some I have been able to catch and throw back. Others have knocked me out of the ballpark. That is where you end up when you are on the wrong track. This track is wide and leads you straight to hell. It is not easy coming back from there. It is an uphill battle the whole way. It is impossible to do it on your own. Hence you need a friend. That person I had been looking for most of my life. That person I could not find. I found some impersonators but never the true friend. I settled for myself. Remember I was the I, I, I, me, me, me person.

I guess my brother Cliff saw the train bearing down on me. He did his best to pull me off the tracks, but I did one better. I ignored his help.

He took me to church. He introduced me to the pastor. I stumbled through some "come join our church" classes, but they were more of a nuisance for me. I had better ways to spend my time, or so I thought. Although I did complete the class and had the opportunity to join, I choose not to. I told Cliff I would join just to make him feel good. He was excited for me. As a gift to me for joining the church, the pastor had purchased a Bible. It was a beautiful white leather-bound Bible. He had my name engraved on the front in gold. I never did get to open it up. I only got to see what I was not going to get. I never joined, and they never gave me the Bible. I think they kept it in hopes I would come to my senses and ask to be forgiven.

The problem with that thought was I did not know to ask for forgiveness. I cannot blame my brother. He did what was asked of him and I just was not ready to accept the invitation. You see, the invitation did not come from Jesus. I can say Cliff was able to plant a seed for Jesus. That seed was watered over the years, and there was a harvest. My sweet brother was a witness. He saw with his own eyes the transformation that took place within me. I thank God that Cliff was able to see what his planting had harvested. It took decades before I understood what Cliff tried so many years ago to help me with.

Today I can say in no uncertain terms I was given an invitation, and I accepted. I thank all those that watered the seed Cliff had planted. I know it took more than a watering to get that seed to grow, but I am thankful for the patience of my Savior. I feel blessed, and all the glory goes to the one true God. My Master, my Savior. To him, I praise each day.

I pray you too will find the friend you have been looking for. He is easy to contact. Just give him a callout. He is waiting to hear from you.

John 15:12–15. My command is this: love each other as I have loved you. Greater love has no one than this, that he lay down his life for his friends. You are my friends if you do what I command. I no longer call you servants because a servant does not know his master's business. Instead, I have called you friends, for everything that I learned from my Father I have made known to you.

Finding Your Quiet

I fight for the moments
Where silence abounds
That is when I hear him
When there are no sounds

He is in my heart
I feel him there
It is so wonderful to know
That he does care

The beat of my heart
Begins to slow
Our souls start to mesh
I feel his glow

There is nothing like it
Being held from within
My soul is so happy
I start to grin

I cherish the moments
He spends with me
This is what life
Is supposed to be

I pray for others
To look for the silence
It is there you will find him
And his guidance

He loves you, sweet child
No need to despair
Go find your quiet
He will be there

Finding Love

No matter where you are
Or what you do
If your sights are on God
All will be new

He listens quietly
Sends his advice
In hopes you will hear
And not pay a price

The gift he is offering
Is one to strive for
Why would you turn away
And shut the door

My mind gets so boggled
Looking around
To those that prefer
To continue to drown

God loves us all
He wishes we loved him
This life we have here
Is just a prelim

With God in our lives
Our heart is at peace
I wish I could help others
Before they cease

I pray for my children
As I sit here today
In hopes that they will never
Have to see a doomsday

It is a day that is promised
To come without warning
I pray they will see
A great new morning

Our God will grant them
A place up high
They must love him now
And say goodbye

Goodbye to an empty life
Without any hope
Go to the arms of the Lord
So they can cope

Lost Sheep

The wolf is disguised
In clothing of sheep
He preys on the lost
He devours the weak

We fear this evil
My God says do not fear
Come close to me
I will appear

I will give you the strength
The courage and wisdom
Your knowledge will grow
You will understand my kingdom

God is the goal
We must achieve
Turn away from the evil
You must start to believe

The world is not our home
It is where we live for a time
Focus on heaven
Begin your climb

With God in our hearts
We will never lose
Evil cannot win
But we must choose

I am not proud of who I was, and I'm certainly not proud of who I am. I am humbled. Truly humbled that Jesus never stopped loving me. I went against God's precious Ten Commandments. Ten out of ten, I desecrated. I committed adultery, I lied, I stole, I ignored God, used his name in vain, believed there was a day set aside for me, and hurt my parents.

I gave Satan a foothold on my life. I handed it to him without even realizing what he was up to. Satan gave me permission to destroy myself, to live a life about me. He used every experience to his advantage.

God has shown me a different version. God protected me. He allowed me to see my experiences differently. He has forgiven me. Oh, I am not off the hook. I still suffer the consequences of my actions. The great thing is now I know to turn to God for his comfort. I hope you find encouragement that there is still time for you to find your comfort.

I wasted forty-five years in the desert. I could have experienced the land of milk and honey. Instead, my choice was to stumble and wander. I was poison to myself. My heart was unforgiving; that took my joy. My Jesus helped me. He took that poison from me. He gave me life in return. He will do the same for you. You need only to respond to his call. He is where grace and mercy reside.

1 John 1:9. If we confess our sins, he is faithful and just and will forgive us our sins and purify us from all unrighteousness.

Proverbs 19:21. Many are the plans in a man's heart, but it is the Lord's purpose that prevails.

Chapter Six

The Division

There is a division in my family. My new life seems to be the cause. Two of my sons have taken the path of this world. The one I had shown them so many years ago. They followed my example. Now as a Christian, Jesus has asked me to spread the gospel. He speaks of hardship for himself as well as his followers in doing so. For years, I was crushed by the isolation of my family, but I cannot relinquish my salvation. Once my eyes were opened, I could see there would be no turning back for me.

My children never leave my mind. I pray daily that God will open their hearts and minds. It is difficult to sit back and watch as your child goes down the same hole as you did. They believe the hole they choose will result in greener pastures. There is only one way out of that hole in good shape. It is God pulling you back through by your feet. You will be bruised and banged up, but those are minor side effects. Our great healer will help you to heal. Continuing down that hole brings much pain and darkness. My old life has been forgiven, but I still feel the pain. It is a consequence I must live with. I passed my old life down to unsuspecting children. As adults now, they have a choice to make. I pray they will follow my example once again. I pray they too will find their salvation. There they will rest in the arms of our Lord and Savior.

John 1:12. Yet to all who received Him, to those who believed in his name, he gave the right to become children of God.

Jeremiah 29:11. For I know the plans I have for you, declares the Lord, plans to prosper you and not to harm you, plans to give you hope and a future.

James 5:6. Therefore confess your sins to each other and pray for each other so that you may be healed. The prayer of the righteous person is powerful and effective.

Mothers

Does a mother ever
Outgrow her role
It is hard to handle
That she has lost her control

She loves her children
Longs for their attention
They are out of her hands
She accepts the rejection

She weeps at night
Prays for their souls
Jesus comes to her side
She he consoles

He brings her peace
Comforts her heart
He helps her from feeling
She is falling apart

She wonders if they ever
Think about her
Has she become noth-
ing to them?
Is she just a blur?

Old age has set in
Her youth is gone
She wants to right
All the wrong

She loves her children
They are a part of her soul
The lives they live now
Are out of her control

Invite

I am not the enemy
The enemy is so proud
He boasts of conceit
He hides out in the crowd

He finds the weak
He preys on their souls
He steals their breath
That is his goal

He comes in the dark
He hates the light
He is slimy and sneaky
As he sends you an invite

Our nation has accepted
What he has offered
It is hard to live here
It has become so awkward

I cry out to God
Good is still here
We are his people
That love him so dear

His work must be done
There is no time to spare
Get on your knees
Send him your prayer

Save who you can
Show them God's way
It is urgent you do this
Before the last day

He Lives

I must confess with my mouth
That Jesus is Lord
What a pleasure it brings me
It is him I adore

I speak quietly at times
And times I shout for joy
For the gift I have been given
No one can destroy

He blessed me with spirit
One I carry in my heart
Only I can mess that up
And set us apart

I will not allow a separation
He is here to stay
He is my Savior, my Lord
One day he will take me away

I look forward to that day
But until it arrives
I will do my best
I will continue to survive

I pray for my family
And generations to come
May they love the Lord Jesus
May this world they overcome

Finding Jesus

Our lives run astray
When our eyes are not open
We must learn to focus
On him we put hope in

He shelters and comforts
He waits for your word
He will never leave you
He wants to be heard

Your heart must be ready
Your ears tuned to hear
The message he sends
Before it disappears

He gave you life
He gave you a choice
He waits for your love
One day you can rejoice

So simple it seems
Makes me wonder why
So many backs are turned
I just want to cry

God bless you, my friends
May you open your hearts
To the love Jesus offers
So you can take part

Chapter Seven

Superhero

My father was my superhero. He knew me from the inside out. His smile brought me pleasure. I always had a fascination about him. His hands were the most intriguing part of him. They were vast and powerful, yet tender and merciful. I love this man. He went home twenty years ago. The worst day, but also the best day of my life.

My dad worked ludicrous hours. He would leave the house by four in the morning to beat the other calf buyers to the many farms in our countryside. It is a trade that has gone by the wayside for the little one-pop business. I remember during the summer, he would let me ride along with him. I didn't care about the hour; I was happiest with him. These were my special days. We would stop at a farm to see if the farmer had any calves for sale. My dad was the best negotiator. The farmer and he would go back and forth about the price. I recall my dad usually got his way. He would load up the calf and off to the next farm. Most all the calves he bought were little black and white ones. I liked them, but they never seemed too special. Then we went to the farm that had an amazing little brown calf. I didn't know at the time calves came brown. I loved this little guy. Dad squabbled back and forth with the farmer trying to purchase him, but the farmer would not come down in price. Next thing I knew, we are getting back in the truck without "Brownie." I was devastated. He was going to be Queeny and my new friend. My tears broke loose; I was heartbroken. We were leaving. Dad stopped and tried to comfort me. He tried to tell a six-year-old that financially, this calf was just not feasible. I didn't care about money. I cared about my new friend. In the end, Dad backed up, and Brownie was in the truck heading home with me.

Dad kept the calves for only a few days. He would fatten them up with milk in hopes of getting the best price for them at market. I loved the brown calf. He went on walks with Queeny and me. He did not listen like Queeny did, but I loved him just the same. Brownie stayed longer than any other calf had ever stayed. He was mine, or at least I thought so.

Market day came again. This time, Brownie got loaded up with the other black and white calves heading to their demise. I jumped in the back of the truck with him, begging Dad to please take him out. I rode all the way to market in the back of the truck with my friend. Upon arrival, all calves were put on the scale together. I couldn't bear to think this was going to be the last time I saw him. Tears were flowing. My Dad could not bear to see me cry, he went down to the scale and lifted Brownie to safety. Brownie spent the next couple of years with Queeny and I. He didn't get to leave the fenced-in portion of our property, but he loved chasing us around when we joined him on his turf.

I am not sure what happened, but money became scarce. The next thing I knew, my home, my serenity, had been sold. We were moving to a two-bedroom apartment. There were still five of us living at home, so our quarters were going to be tight. I began to worry about Brownie; where was he going to live? I didn't worry about Queeny. She was my friend and would just stay in my bed with me.

Moving day came, and a red truck rolled up our driveway. I figured Dad had found some help to move our things. They moved some things but not what I was thinking. Brownie was leaving. I hung onto him as long as I could. I know he was crying too. The sounds he made broke my heart. That was the last day I got to see Brownie. He was an amazing friend while I had him.

I went on the first trip with furniture to our new home. I stayed at the apartment, helping mom unpack and organize. It was late in the evening when Dad finally arrived with the last load. I knew he must have Queeny with him. I ran out to his truck calling her. Dad looked like he had just lost his best friend. He picked me up with his massive hands and told me Queeny went to live with Jesus. What? Who is this Jesus guy, and why did he have my friend? Dad said she was old, eighteen to be exact, and she was worn out. I could not believe what I was hearing. I did not even get the chance to tell her goodbye. I wondered if she was as confused as I was. I spent the next several months crying myself to sleep on my rollaway bed in the middle of the living room floor. I thought maybe Jesus would get tired of her and bring her home to me, because she must have been sad just like me. Jesus certainly was not my friend. When I asked where he lived, Dad would tell me in a faraway place. He said one day I would get to go there and spend time with him. He told me Queeny didn't hurt anymore, but I just didn't understand. I was still hurting. How could she not miss me and hurt like I did?

Dad was changing. He seemed not to have time for me. Mom and he fought daily. He would leave early in the morning and not come home till the early hours of the next day. The fights were enormous on those nights. I now understand he had demons tormenting his mind. The calf business had gone away. He had no job. The alcoholic demons were running a full course within my dad.

Many nights, I would hear his truck coming a mile away. His exhaust was so loud as he drove home like a wild man. I would cringe knowing in a few minutes, my restful sleep was over. He would stumble up the steps only to have mom waiting. The vocabulary got colorful at this point. He was not going to allow mom to shame him. He was going to leave and go back to the bar.

I became the referee. I would start out trying to calm him down. Then came the pleading and more begging to get him to stay. I loved him. I wanted him to be safe. I wanted my daddy back. Slowly, every night, I could see his own disappointment in his face. It would surface as if he knew what he was doing to us. I would get his keys from him, help him to the recliner. He would sleep off his booze in that chair.

Eventually he sobered up, got a truck driving job. Now he could once again support us. He was back, my superhero. I blocked out those years of the alcohol. I never wanted to remember him like that. He wasn't anyone I knew. His demons took so much of his life and my childhood.

My dad aged with grace. His family was his life. The grandchildren were the prize. He loved each and every one of us with his whole heart. There was never a time when I would visit that he did not jump from his chair to come share a huge hug and kiss. I always got an "I love you" when coming and going. He was back in full force.

As he aged, his memory became less and less. He struggled for words to form simple sentences, but he always knew me. That was a blessing. About four years before he passed, things were bad. Mom would have to lock the door from the inside so he could not get out and wander away. We did spend several occasions scanning the neighborhood when he got out by himself. He loved walking. It broke my heart that he was locked inside most days. That is when I made the decision to stop working. Mom and Dad became the focus of my day. Dad and I would spend hours just walking. That seemed to give him life, a purpose.

I remember one day we were walking, and he stopped me. His face changed and he said, "Angel, I know what's happening. It's difficult to explain but I'm going to be just fine." Just that fast, he slipped back into his own world. I was sad but also elated that I got that moment with him. My superhero was still inside. It brought joy to my heart.

I spent four years, every day, doing the same routine. David and I didn't go anywhere. I didn't want to leave my dad. One night, I received a call from Mom. Dad had a stroke. We drove him to the hospital. He spent one week there and was then sent to a rehabilitation center. For the next two weeks, I would arrive early and leave late.

The Chicago boat show was in full swing. David asked if we could please just take a few hours for ourselves and go. I agreed it would probably do me good. We stopped for a late lunch before going to see Dad. I received a devastating call from Mom. She said Dad was bad, deteriorating fast. She said I needed to get there as fast as I could. It took about an hour to reach the nursing home. Dad had already slipped into a coma. My siblings were all around him. I was angry at each of them. I spent four years every day with Dad, and now they got to say goodbye and I didn't. How could this possibly be fair? There was a lot of small talk amongst them. I just remember holding that massive hand between mine. I could not believe I was about to lose my superhero. Little by little, family came in and family left. Around midnight, it was just Mom, my sister Linda, my brother Denny, and myself left to sit with him. I warned the others Dad did not have much time left, but they said they would be back early. I continued holding that precious hand. (Sometimes I can still feel him holding my hand.) About five in the morning, I could hardly hold my head up. I had taken my jacket off and stuffed it under my head to take a little nap in the chair beside Dad's bed. I started praying. I had never prayed before. I was not sure if there was a right way or wrong way, but I remember pleading with God. I asked for just one more chance to tell my Dad I loved him. I did not want him to leave without those words going with him. I asked God to open his eyes to let him see me. I needed him to know he was my superhero.

It is difficult to explain what happened next. At the time, I had no idea what was going on. The truth is God delivered on my asking. I saw myself asleep in that chair next to Dad's bed, with my red winter coat under my head. I was above my dad's body. I did not feel like I was floating. I was just there. I looked straight ahead, and I saw him, my dad at my level above the bed. He smiled; he was so handsome. He no longer looked frail and beaten. He was new. We exchanged our love, one that lives on in me to this day. His death from this world led me to a new life. The promise of an eternal life with God the Father. I knew God had given to me a miracle.

I sat up in that chair as his body expelled air for the last time. My daddy went home.

John 10:28–30. I give them eternal life, and they shall never perish; no one can snatch them out of my hand. My Father, who has given them to me, is greater than all; no one can snatch them out of my Father's hand. I and the Father are one.

Daddy

I sit beside
My daddy's bed
My heart is heavy
As if it were led

I hold his massive hand
I hold it between mine
I think of the times
It has been so kind

I cannot believe
His time has come
His leaving has certainly
Made me numb

I close my eyes
Down my cheeks come the tears
Today is the day
My heart has feared

So many memories
Rush my mind
I realize that I am
The one left behind

I whisper softly
Into his ear
I love you, Daddy
You are so dear

I prayed to God
To let him speak
To be my rock
So things would not be bleak

My God in heaven
Needed daddy now
He granted me a wish
But I do not know how

My soul took a journey
Outside my vessel
I saw a healthy man
Headed to somewhere special

I will never forget
The glimpse I was given
For now, I know
My daddy had risen

Daddy's Pennies

When you left this world
You broke my heart
Each day it gets better
Even though we are apart

I got your message
The one you sent last night
It woke me up late
I smiled with delight

Our God is so awesome
He knows what I need
Just a penny from heaven
Helps me to proceed

Some days my body
Just goes through the motion
It looks so normal
But it really lacks emotion

Those are the days
He sends you to me
I cannot praise him enough
For setting me free

Because of his Son
We both have been saved
We took the path
That he has paved

One day, my sweet Daddy
We will need the pen-
nies no more
We will spend our days in heaven
Praising our Lord

Because of Jesus

By faith I have lived
I rejoice now in sight
Jesus called my name
He showed me the light

My pain is gone
No sadness here
Just rejoicing in love
That is so sincere

I am not alone
He brought me to heaven
It is a reward for my faith
Oh, what a blessing

I will wait by the gate
To help you someday
But meanwhile live
Understand it is okay

Our worlds are different
But the love is the same
God's promise to us
Will never change

My life was a blessing
You loved me so much
I can still hear you
Just keep in touch

To my family I love
Your faith you must keep
It is the ticket for you
To make your final leap

Designer

God is the designer
Of each of us
In him we can trust
And not have to fuss

He gave us this world
For our comfort and peace
With him at our side
We will never cease

There is a home awaiting
For us in the sky
Jesus will bring us home
So we'll never die

Imagine that day
As you kneel before him
Knowing it is the Lord
That has washed away your
sin

My prayer is for all
To see that day
It is a day there'll be nothing
You have to say

Give thanks to the Lord
He is your goal
He is your true constant
That will save your soul

Chapter Eight

The Delay

I spearheaded a cruise for ten couples. We arrived in Galveston the evening before the cruise. I had everything planned and laid out. Things were falling into place just like I expected.

At seven thirty, the morning of the cruise, I received a call from the cruise line. There was going to be a several-hour delay because of the fog. The lobby of the hotel was packed with many unhappy cruisers.

I needed to get away from all the complaining. David and I took a walk. About ten minutes into our walk, I spotted him. I knew in no uncertain terms he was the reason for the delay.

That may sound confusing to a reasonable person. For me, it was just another one of those days; those days God uses me to get his plan completed. I have given God control of me; I surrender my life to him. Retired Private William Jensen of the United States Army was my soon-to-be mission.

I watched and waited for him to cross the street. He was disheveled, and it appeared it had been some time since he saw a shower. As he got closer, I could smell the alcohol on his breath and body.

I smiled, reached out my hand, and introduced myself as he stepped onto the sidewalk. He immediately gave me his name and rank. He said he was a Vietnam veteran. I listened as he told me about his last week in Vietnam. His face told his story. He was still living in his past. My heart broke for this man. I asked if I could pray for him. He immediately responded yes. I took hold of him. I touched my head to his. I prayed, and we both wept. It was such a humbling experience for me. As I started to step back, he said he had not been touched in over fifteen years. How unimaginable is that.

God has given to me different eyes and a different heart. My eyes and heart look for the unloved, lost, and those that are alone. I was once a loner, and I felt unloved. Now I get to see things others do not. I see from within me. I used to think being a loner as a child and young adult was a burden. What I have learned is it is a blessing. You have heard of a blessing in disguise? That is what it is.

I am pulled to the person begging for help on the street corner. I promised God I would never go by anyone and not offer help, a prayer, and a touch. It took years of feeling alone to have eyes to see into the heart of a loner. I am thankful for my past because it has given me a humbled present. I am blessed by every touch of the unloved.

Revelation 21:4. "And God will wipe away every tear from their eyes; there shall be no more death, nor sorrow, nor crying. There shall be no more pain, for the former things have passed away."

Vitamins F.A.I.T.H.

F.A.I.T.H. are the vitamins
Needed to survive
When your heart is lacking
These vitamins will keep you alive

F is for the Father
The creator of all
He'll show you the way
You don't have to fall

A is for ascend
Up into the sky
Our Savior did that
Now we will never die

I is for immune
Protected from all evil
Hearts will be at peace
You will not be in upheaval

T is for tomb
Where our Savior was placed
He arose from there
With so much grace

H is for heaven
Our home we long for
Our Savior will come get us
Our new home we will adore

Delivered

Where did I lead me?
Have I been to hell?
Have I found my way back?
These questions will
help me propel

I have lived in darkness
A choice that I had made
Many scary things live there
It is time I make a trade

Freedom is not free
It is a choice I must make
The stakes are life or death
God is the choice I must take

I traded the darkness for light
It is the only way to go
I see my Jesus everywhere
He helps me continue to grow

His plan is perfect
He made one just for me
I struggle daily to
know what's right
Oh God, help me to see

I cannot see my future
Or the end of my path
I know I must move forward
And escape all the wrath

Psalm 36 Reminder

His love endures forever
No matter my mistake
He gave me life and breath
He only asks I partake

My heart is to share
The joy it has received
With souls that are lost
They will no longer be deceived

So many are wounded
So many cannot see
I pray to my God
I can help them be set free

Satan works overtime
To beat me down
But my God holds me up
He will not let me hit the ground

When Satan hits me
And I go to my knees
He thinks he is winning
But it is God that I please

Punches from Satan
Bring me to prayer
He cannot win God's child
That is hard for him to bear

The punches get harder
As the years go by
What he does not understand
I do not want to die

I fight for my life
I will fight for you too
It is a choice I've made
We can be new

Home is in heaven
That is where we belong
I will fight this battle
I will stay strong.

History

I never liked history
Just a bunch of old words
Did not apply to me
They seemed so absurd

My thoughts have changed
I now realize
Without those old words
I could not become wise

God gave me his Word
In the oldest book yet
I read it and read it
To stop all the fret

It is amazing how time
Repeats itself
God's Word is there
To change oneself

God sent many prophets
To save his people
But they turned back
To their very own evil

History repeats
I see it in print
I cannot understand
Why we do not take the hint

God sent us the best
Gift of all
It is right in his book
For us to recall

It is his Son he sent
To save us this day
He will conquer the evil
That comes our way

Chapter Nine

The Baptism

Just because we find our faith does not mean trouble will leave our lives. What it means is we will handle it differently. God tells us to pray without ceasing. Prayer gives us strength to overcome this world. It was exactly what I was going to need.

David and I moved about 1 1/2 hours away from our church. We found it difficult to be engaged in weekly studies, so we went church shopping. That may sound crazy, but we felt it important to find a church that believed in all biblical principles. We needed a church that preached God's Word fully intact.

We thought we found the right one. It felt like home. We helped, we shared, we learned, and we grew in our faith. The summer of 2014, David and I were compelled to be baptized. We wrote our testimonies and were prepared to share them.

It felt good to finally have the chance to shed my past in public. I had come to know our Lord in 2000 but never shared my testimony with family and friends. I was excited to be part of this wonderful experience. I did not hold back. I spoke about the old me. The more I spoke, the lighter my heart became. I was totally free of my dark past. No more hiding, no more being afraid someone would find out who I had been. I spilled it all through many tears, but it ended with a smile.

It was a day I will never forget. It seems it gave me a bigger heart. I had more room in it for others. My focus was on "the church." I wanted to do the job God had given me and do it with grace. I found myself always looking to see the needs of others. I wanted to work outside the walls of the physical church building.

At a woman's ministry meeting, I shared my thoughts. I had laid out a plan for us to work with those less fortunate than ourselves. It was about giving back and sharing our Jesus. I could not imagine that there was anything wrong with the plan. It is my understanding the plan was good; it was who delivered the idea that led to so much turmoil. My mentor, our leader, looked at me in that meeting and said that I had not walked with Jesus long enough to be of help. She pushed the idea aside and continued with the meeting. After the meeting, I asked her to point me to the scripture that would tell me how long it would take before I was usable. She was unhappy with my questioning of her authority. She shared her concern with the elder board. I was so confused as to what was happening. I was reprimanded for questioning her decision. I was summoned to a meeting with the elders, the pastor, and my mentor. During the meeting, she explained to me that my past, my testimony, was tainted, and I needed time to grow. I had been with Christ for some fourteen years; I did mission work in Tanzania, Africa, for four years during that period. Yet she stated again that I was not usable. I am not sure what that meant, but after four hours going around and around in that meeting listening to my past being replayed, I excused myself as politely as possible and went home to cry and pray.

There was nothing else humanly possible for me to do. Prayer was my answer. Prayer does not always give you the outcome you are looking for, but it will give you the direction that is needed. God provides when you ask. I was asking for his help and guidance.

I was not sure if I belonged anymore. I could feel the loneliness start to settle in my heart. I could not let them take my joy. Better yet, I could not give them my joy.

I lived in prayer, constant prayer, asking for direction. Do I stay and turn the other cheek, or do I go find somewhere new? I wanted it to be God's choice, not mine.

That very week, God placed the answer before me. I was given an invitation to a newly planted church from a stranger in a setting unfamiliar to either of us. It was only God that could have provided the circumstance in which we met. It was God's answer. I had work waiting for me somewhere else. God gave me a choice, but it was clear the direction I needed to take. Two days after meeting Gwen, David and I accepted her invitation. We found our new church home.

People that heard my story have said "church" people are hypocrites. They state that is why they do not go to church. I pray for them. I pray one day they will overcome their fear of church. Things happen for a reason. I was needed somewhere else. God needed my attention. He certainly got it. The issue was not how long I had walked with Jesus; it was about how well I would listen.

We are all sinners and need to be forgiven. Did I feel things could have been handled better? Yes, but it was not about my feelings. It was about God's plan. I pray for my old mentor, that her eyes are now open. I pray she leads and does not discourage. I grew from this trial. I thank God for being with me every step of the way. This trial was not about me. It was about a future God already had planned.

Psalm 46:1. God is our refuge and strength. A very present help in trouble. Therefore, we will not fear.

Titus 3:5. He saved us, not because of righteous things we had done, but because of his mercy.

Going Under

The future's not mine
The past is lost
What I do in the present
Comes with a cost

I learned that thought
On the day I was dipped
Into the water
To become equipped

Jesus watched me go under
Full of much sin
He brought me to the surface
To stop what I was engaged in

He opened my ears
To hear his sweet voice
What I have heard from him
Is I have a choice

I choose his love
His kindness and grace
Living for oneself
Leaves you in last place

I pray for others
That think God's wrong
They think on the last day
They will stand strong

He sends us lifelines
Every day of our lives
In hope we listen
And want to survive

I thank God every day
For his hand of mercy
My mind is clear
There is no controversy

There is only one God
The creator of all
He is waiting for you
To give him a call

Time

God is the giver of time
Have I been wise with
what I have been given?
The responsibility is mine
That is what he has written

I have chosen badly
More than I care to remember
It is time to get on board
To enjoy all his splendor

He controls all things
Even when I think I do
My moments from now on
Must be about the pursue

My every thought
Oh God must be of you
You will teach my heart
A different view

The earthly things
Will wither away
The love you have for me
Will shine on the Lord's day

The Lord will arrive in glory
My heart will leap for joy
The wicked will be gone
Satan he will destroy

Time will never matter
Days will not exist
Nothing about this earth
Will ever be missed

Heaven will be my home
God will be my master
I will be filled with love
No more disaster

Time still exists
In the here and now
Give your life to Jesus
Please make that vow

I cannot save you
It is a choice you must make
Please don't hesitate too long
That will be a mistake

Jesus is standing by
He is waiting for you today
Turn away from evil
I pray you don't delay

Where Is She?

She thought tomorrow
Was so far away
Until she looked
Into the mirror today

She is not sure where
The girl has gone
She has not seen her
For so awfully long

The eyes she sees
Have lost their shine
Seems her face
Only has lines

The years went by
Lickity-split
Still not sure
If she is equipped

She studied the Bible
Lived by the Word
But the world she lives in
Is so absurd

She has been faithful
Given her all
So someday soon
She will get the call

As the clouds open up
The trumpets do blare
The Lord up in heaven
Will arrive in the air

He will look into her eyes
That will now shine
He will give to her
The perfect sign

To get on aboard
Leave this world behind
She is headed to a new home
It is much more kind

Now she looks in the mirror
For the very last time
The girl is now back
Without any lines

My Precious Mother

Twice in my life
I have been born
Once to my mother
Once to conform

She brought me to life
Showed me God's path
Many of times
We certainly did clash

But the seed of Christ
She planted in me
It took some time
For me to agree

With Christ at my side
I see all she has done
She is the woman I love
Oh how I've won

She held me so close
When I was small
She picked me up
When I took a fall

She has always been there
Through the laughs and the tears
She stands above all
No one compares

To God I give thanks
For this mother of mine
She stepped up for him
Kept me in line

Because of you, Mom
Our lives will go on
Into eternity
And far beyond

I love you so much
You live in my heart
It is a place God made
We will never be apart

Chapter Ten

One Body

Accepting Jesus Christ as my Lord and Savior brought a new concept to my life. I now belonged to the "one body." The body of Christ. As a loner, that concept was overwhelming to me. How does a loner become part of the local body of Christ as well as the universal body of Christ? It takes steps, a lot of them. It takes wisdom, God's wisdom, to understand.

I have had many questions about where I fit. I've been told by mentors and pastors what my gifts are. How could they know if I had no idea myself? How can man know what God has given to individuals as a gift if that individual is not practicing their given talents? I've been told I'm a leader, a disrupter, a dreamer, an organizer, but what I see is whatever the local body needed, I fit the bill. What I have learned is my place within the body is a gift from God, one only he and I know. You cannot function as a leg if you are an eye. I cannot be put into a peg that was not made for me no matter the need. More important to where I fit in the body is my connection to Christ. It is through Christ, in Christ, that I have been attached as "one body."

I can still be a loner but part of the "one body." Remember as a small child I was always looking for something? I was looking for a friend. I was looking for the next job. I was looking for the next adventure, and looking, looking, and looking. The eyes I have been given are always looking. As I journeyed on this trip back into my past, I can now see God was preparing my sight for the future, to glorify him. God gave me sight that is different than most. I struggle with my sight, for I have the ability to see deeply into others. I can feel what I see. I see the unloved for I have been unloved. I see the poor for I have been poor. I see the wicked for I have been wicked. I see the lonely for I have been lonely. I see the liar for I have been one. Sometimes it seems sight can be a curse, but it is a gift from God, so I feel blessed with my gift. Now for the challenge. How do I share what I see with those that have no sight? Being part of one body isn't always easy, but it is our lifeline to move the gospel forward. Learning each other's gifts and working together with a pure heart will create a body of unity. This world has become so dark, it's time we act as "one body." We must share our talents. Some talents may seem harsh, but if applied in a godly manner for the purpose of building the "one body," we will overcome this world and the darkness within.

At sixty-seven years old, I am still learning and growing. God gave me feet to move forward, not to stand still. We, as the body, must never stop learning and growing. We must use our gifts to help others achieve what God has for them. Darkness cannot stop us, for Christ's light is within us. He is our compass, the one and only one to lead us on his righteous path.

I had a problem with looking and being different until I was introduced to Jesus. He said the one body is not about looking the same. It is about all the differences. God did not refer to our color, nationality, financial status, age, intellect, or any other differences within us. He referenced one thing—the love for Christ. It is the love for Jesus Christ that makes us one. I see people struggle with nationality and color more than anything. It is Satan's way to keep us from being "one body." People that see my color are not part of the "one body." They may be sitting on the outside of the body feeling they are attached, but if they continue to see me as an individual, they will suffer, and I will suffer. Unity is our defense against Satan.

We, as the body, have had many challenges and will continue to have more. If we, the body, cannot come together, this world will continue to do what it is doing. The world is doing everything possible to play out what God has already shown us to be true in his Word. We are not given the day or hour Christ will return, but we are on the path to his return sooner than what you may have anticipated.

Hatred and greed are at the forefront of our everyday lives. We speak many words, but are they the right words? Are we sharing the gospel? It is my job as well as yours to complete God's mission with love. We must love our enemy and use the strength of one body to do so. If we stand in unity, our God will provide all we need, and one day as we stand firm for the Lord, a reward will be given.

Matthew 25:23. His Master replied, "Well done, good and faithful servant! You have been faithful with a few things; I will put you in charge of many things. Come and share your master's happiness!"

One Body

If I am only half attached
I will let the body down
I will not be strong
   to carry burdens
My Lord will surely frown

     We must recruit more feet
     To keep us standing strong
     It is the job we were given
     We must not do it wrong

   I was given a place
When Jesus set me free
This place comes with
     expectations
For both you and me

     Obedience comes with a price
     Sometimes it causes pain
     It is only for a short time
     Then heaven we will obtain

In weakness I do tremble
I do not want to damage you
Generations can fall and stumble
We must stay strong to
   help them through

     I pray for the body
     Please do your job
     Let's achieve God's goal
So generations will not be robbed

   We are one body
We cry for the feet are gone
It is difficult for us to stand
When they have now withdrawn

Invasion

My space becomes invaded
By Satan and his mob
The mighty fight ensues
I must do my job

I stand for God
I give him my all
I do what is best
He's made it my call

The fight is fierce
The stakes are high
It is life versus death
It cannot be a tie

My mind must be focused
One hundred percent
On God and his word
To stop the torment

God whispers gently
Into my ear
The loud noise all around
I must not hear

The control in his voice
Is what I need
It gives me strength
So evil cannot succeed

I fight for my family
Every second of the day
I must never loosen up
I must keep evil at bay

My body is so weary
It's tired from the fight
God gives me the rest I need
By shinning his light

His light is warm
It melts my fear
He holds me close at night
Wipes away my tear

I pray for his strength
To get me through today
Must not worry about tomorrow
That is the Lord's way.

Judgement Day

What words will I hear
On the great judgment day
Have I been deceitful
Or did I obey?

Will salvation be mine?
Was my heart pure with love?
Did I give to others?
Did they feel unloved?

My heart is the clue
To all my questions
Was I faithful, dear God?
Did I absorb your lessons?

A short nineteen inches
From my mind to my heart
Was that circuit complete
Or was it apart?

As years flash by
My heart and mind
Have certainly tried to be
One of a kind

My heart is my spirit
My mind is my soul
With God's heavenly connection
He is forever in control

I have peace in abundance
I have love that is pure
My body, my soul, my spirit
Have now become mature

That final day is coming
But now I can rest
For my God knows all
He knows I did my best

# About the Author

Kim Olson was cofounder of Zawadi ni Zawadi, a Christian nonprofit organization meaning a "a gift is a gift." She worked in Tanzania and Kenya, Africa, providing financial assistance to children so they could obtain a Christian education. She worked on the ground, building a library to help the children to see beyond their own country. The organization supplied books and school supplies from gracious donors throughout the United States. In the United States, she was founder of Salute Ministries out of Lake County, Illinois. She assisted homeless veterans move from the streets to a furnished home with items she and her husband worked tirelessly to find through donations. Move-in days were their opportunity to share Christ with the men and woman that had lost their way. She now runs the Reality of Mercy Street Ministry as an evangelist spreading the great news of our Lord and Savior Jesus Christ. She made a promise to God never to walk away from someone asking for help on the street. That promise has given the lost, lonely, hurting, and unloved an opportunity to find their way home. Each experience has humbled her and given her a closer relationship to the Father. She was once given an opportunity to find her way, to change her life, and she wants everyone to understand who Christ is and what he has to offer them.

CPSIA information can be obtained
at www.ICGtesting.com
Printed in the USA
BVHW090212290721
613102BV00020B/1130